"The true test of leadership is to help others grow."
Harriet Beecher Stowe

LEADERSHIP AND GROWTH
THE VISIONARY ENTREPRENEUR'S BOOK

BY: RŪMĪ ABDOŪLATĪF

CONTENTS

Introduction: The Path of Entrepreneurship

A Way to the Progress

My Journey

A Leader in Motion

Chapter 1: Entrepreneurial Strategy

Creating a Vision and an Action Plan

Different Business Models

Adapting to Market Changes

Chapter 2: Growth and Expansion

How to Drive Business Growth

Entering New Markets

Networking and Strategic Partnerships

Chapter 3: Operations and Efficiency

Optimizing Processes and Systems

Time and Resource Management

The Importance of Productivity

Chapter 4: Marketing and Sales.

Digital and Traditional Marketing Strategies

Effective Sales Techniques

Building a Sustainable Brand

Chapter 5: Finance and Funding

Financial Management and Accounting

Raising Capital and Financing Expansion

The Art of Investment

Chapter 6: Leadership and Team.

How to Inspire and Lead a Team

Recruiting and Retaining Talent

Creating a Positive Company Culture

A big thank you to Nathalie Donovan and Hedgardt H. Graham for all their guidance. Also, to my family for always being my greatest supporters.

INTRODUCTION
THE PATH OF ENTREPRENEURSHIP

"Your place will always be alongside those warm and bold souls who experience glorious victories."
Rūmī Abdoūlatīf

Entrepreneurship is much more than just a path to creating a successful business or building and maintaining a family. It is a quest for constant personal improvement, an experience that pushes one to explore their own limits, reinvent their vision of life, and discover the depths of their potential. Leadership and Growth: The Visionary Entrepreneur's book aims to provide concrete tools and proven strategies for those who wish to embark on this great adventure. But beyond that, this book's mission is to inspire, motivate, and remind you that as visionary entrepreneurs, you are also the creators of your own destiny.

My personal journey is a living example of this. In 2016, I made a radical decision: to distance myself from my loved ones for a time, a time during which I hoped and still hope, through the blessing of the creative source to have the power to be and remain in a constant process of improvement, every day and in every way. This desire for excellence guided me to leave my home country (France) for England, where I had to learn a new language, find a job, and begin investing heavily in myself.

In 2019, life took an unexpected turn. After losing my job, I found myself in the category of the homeless, and I remained there for three and a half years. Those difficult years certainly shaped my character and strengthened my resilience, but they also brought me to rock bottom. The vast majority of the decisions I made during this challenging time proved to be wrong, as they led me into Wandsworth prison, a situation that could have permanently broken many people.

However, throughout my life, I have always considered myself a valuable man, a man of great worth, and I believe today that this kind of reflection is the cornerstone that refines and sustains the character and leadership of visionary entrepreneurs. In prison, I discovered stoicism and meditation through reading, two disciplines that greatly enriched my life. Rather than succumbing to bitterness and despair, I chose to see this imprisonment as an opportunity. I studied, meditated, and began writing what would become my first book: (9 Keys to Access the Circle of Winners), which I published on Amazon a few months after my release from prison. This book was accompanied by several notes on stoicism titled (The Codes of Stoicism: The Black Book). This work marked a turning point in my life. It synthesised everything I had learned: the Stoic principles of great philosophers such as Seneca and Marcus Aurelius, as well as concrete lessons on personal and professional development.

Thus, Leadership and Growth is not the result of direct

entrepreneurial experience—at least not yet—but rather the culmination of an entire mental and philosophical journey, an inner quest. I aimed to create a practical guide for future entrepreneurs, but also a manual that respects the raw reality of failures, challenges, and rebirths. Because, in the end, entrepreneurship is not just an economic exercise: it is a personal revolution, a quest to realise one's dreams, sometimes against all odds. In Leadership and Growth, you will find strategies for running a business, but also reflections on the inner growth necessary to become a true visionary entrepreneur. My ambition with this manual is to provide you with practical tools while encouraging you to draw from your own experiences, to transform failures into opportunities, and to realise that every step, even the most difficult, can bring you closer to great successes. In this Visionary Entrepreneur's book, I share with you everything I have learned and experienced through my readings and personal experiences, with the hope that it will serve you as well.

CHAPTER 1
ENTREPRENEURIAL STRATEGY

"There is nothing more powerful than an idea whose time has come."

Victor Hugo

One of the first steps in any entrepreneurial adventure is to define a clear and effective strategy. Without a strategy, even a brilliant idea runs the risk of remaining a dream. A good strategy is not just a roadmap; it is a guide for navigating an uncertain landscape filled with challenges but also great opportunities.

It all starts with a vision. The most successful entrepreneurs do not merely have an idea for a product or service; they have a precise vision of what their business can become and the impact it can have on the market and society. A strong vision is not limited to a mere aspiration or ambitious dreams. It must be concrete and accompanied by clear direction: where do you want to take your business? How do you see its evolution in five or ten years?

Take the example of Thomas Edison, in my view one of the greatest inventors and entrepreneurs of all time.

Edison did not just seek to invent revolutionary products; he had a vision of how his inventions would change people's everyday lives. When he invented the electric bulb (while knowing that other inventors contributed to this achievement), his goal was not merely to create a source of light but to establish a complete electrical system that could be installed in homes around the world. This integrated vision not only allowed Edison to design the bulb but also to build a business capable of producing and distributing electricity.

The first question that every visionary entrepreneur must answer is: what problem are you solving? Successful businesses are those that offer a concrete solution to a real problem. This problem can be large or small, but it must have perceived value to the customer. Too often, entrepreneurs fall into the trap of developing a product or service without asking whether there is a real need for it.

Consider the example of Henry Ford. Before founding the Ford Motor Company, Ford had a simple yet revolutionary vision: he wanted to make the car accessible to everyone. At that time, cars were luxury items, reserved for the wealthy. Ford identified the problem: car production was too costly and too slow. In response, he developed mass production techniques, such as the assembly line, which reduced costs and allowed cars to be manufactured more quickly. Through this approach, Ford not only succeeded in solving a technical problem but also transformed an entire market.

Another key question in developing your strategy is: what makes your product unique? In other words, what is your unique value proposition? Alternatively, we can rephrase this question as: what sets you apart from the competition? In a saturated market, it is crucial to have something that differentiates your product or service. This could be a specific feature, exceptional customer service, an innovative business model, or even a particular brand positioning.

If you look at companies like Apple, their success largely rests on their unique value proposition. While other tech companies focused on technical specifications and raw performance, Apple concentrated on user experience, design, and ease of use. Their vision was to create technological products that were both powerful and accessible to everyone. This approach allowed Apple to differentiate itself from the competition and build a trusted brand.

Rigidity is the enemy of growth in a constantly changing economic environment. A good strategy is not just about establishing a fixed plan but adopting a flexible mindset that allows you to adjust direction as conditions evolve. Markets, customer needs, and technologies change rapidly, and the companies that succeed are those that know how to adapt.

One of the most striking examples is Nokia. In the 1990s, Nokia was the global leader in mobile phones. However, as smartphones emerged and consumers began seeking multifunctional devices, Nokia failed to adapt its strategy to this new reality. In contrast, companies like Samsung and Apple quickly responded by developing products that met these new needs, allowing them to capture a significant market share. The lesson here is simple: one must be ready to adjust their strategy to meet new market demands.

In addition to flexibility, it is essential to keep an eye on the competition. How do you outpace your competitors? It's not just about offering a better product but also understanding the market, anticipating competitors' moves, and ensuring that you are in a strong position to react. For this, competitive analysis is crucial. You need to know the strengths and weaknesses of your competitors, as well as identify market opportunities they might overlook.

A great example here is Jeff Bezos, the founder of Amazon. Bezos has always been obsessed with competition, but in a particular way: he does not seek to follow them but to innovate beyond them. Amazon focused on user experience, rapid expansion, and logistical efficiency, which allowed them to outpace their competitors not only on price but also on service quality.

Finally, an often-overlooked aspect of entrepreneurial strategy is the exit strategy. Knowing from the outset how you envision the end of your entrepreneurial journey can influence many decisions along the way. Do you want to sell your business one day? Pass it on to your children?

Focus on an IPO (initial public offering)? These questions may seem distant, but they are crucial for determining how to structure and grow your business.

In terms of entrepreneurial strategy, it is essential to understand that the path to success is neither linear nor predictable. Entrepreneurs must constantly adapt to a rapidly changing environment. But if there is one aspect that remains immutable, it is the ability to identify opportunities where others may only see obstacles. This is where the concept of the unique value proposition (UVP) comes into play.

Every entrepreneur must be able to answer this question clearly and convincingly: what makes your product unique once again? The unique value proposition (UVP) is what distinguishes a company from its competitors and compels a customer to choose your product or service over another. The most successful companies are those that can articulate a UVP that directly addresses the needs and desires of their target audience. Take the example of a company positioned in a saturated market. On the surface, the product or service offered might not differ much from that of competitors. But what makes the difference is the ability to communicate this value in a way that captures attention and resonates with customers.

In the early 20th century, Madam C.J. Walker, a black American woman, became the most successful entrepreneur of her time by creating a line of hair care products for Black women. She transformed her passion into a business opportunity while solving a problem that many others hadn't even noticed. At a time when hair care products were non-existent for Black women, she understood that meeting this specific need would place her in a position of strength. Her business thrived because she successfully translated her UVP into a message that was relevant to an often-overlooked community.

Madam Walker not only built a business empire but also inspired future generations by demonstrating that the key to success lies in a thorough understanding of market needs and the ability to create innovative solutions.

Beyond the importance of the value proposition, another essential facet of entrepreneurial strategy is competitive analysis. Companies operate in complex ecosystems where new players constantly emerge, and entrepreneurs must find ways not only to stand out but also to outperform their competitors.

This starts with a deep understanding of your competitors, especially their weaknesses. Many fail by trying to replicate what already works in other companies, without asking if there might be a better way. Your strategy should always aim to fill gaps left by the competition. So, how do you beat the competition?

Instead of simply creating a powerful phone, Steve Jobs identified that consumers wanted more than a phone: they wanted an intuitive, simple tool that would revolutionise how they communicate and interact with the world. The iPhone wasn't just an innovative product; it was a new way to conceive the phone.

Another approach to staying ahead of your competitors is to invest in continuous innovation. Companies often stagnate when they rest on their laurels and fail to explore new horizons. However, successful entrepreneurs are those who continue to innovate, even after securing a significant share of the market. Finally, a wise entrepreneur knows that adaptability is crucial. Markets change rapidly under the influence of many factors: consumer trends, new technologies, and even global economic shifts. Those who fail are often the ones who cling too tightly to a rigid strategy, unable to pivot when circumstances require it.

In its early days, Netflix focused on renting DVDs by mail. But over time, it understood that the future of content consumption lay in streaming. By embracing this new technological direction, Netflix not only survived but dominated a transforming market. Its agility in anticipating shifts in consumer behavior and adapting quickly allowed it to surpass giants like Blockbuster, which clung too tightly to an outdated model.

For entrepreneurs who have already established a solid foundation in their local market, global expansion is a natural strategic step to consider. However, venturing internationally is not a decision to be taken lightly. This process requires not only rigorous preparation but also the ability to understand the cultural, economic, and legal specificities of the new target markets.

One of the main advantages of a global expansion

strategy is the opportunity to access new customer segments, increase brand awareness, and diversify revenue sources. However, it also requires adapting products or services to meet cultural preferences and local regulations. Companies that succeed internationally are those that can maintain their identity while adapting to the specific needs of each region.

A classic example of success in global expansion is Coca-Cola. Though universally recognised, the company has managed to tailor its products and marketing strategy to fit local cultures. In some countries, recipes have been adjusted to suit local tastes, while in others, advertising campaigns have focused on specific cultural values. This flexible but cohesive approach has enabled Coca-Cola to become one of the most successful brands in the world.

As crucial as expansion strategy may be, no business can succeed without a strong and committed team. As an entrepreneur, your role is not limited to managing finances or strategic planning. You must also be the leader who inspires and guides your team toward achieving set goals.

One of the keys to building a team capable of supporting growth is to recruit people who share your vision and values. While technical skills are essential, company culture is equally important. Employees should feel motivated by the company's mission and be prepared to adapt to constantly evolving environments. This means investing in training and professional development must be a priority.

Another critical aspect is managing talent on a global

scale. When expanding internationally, it is often necessary to recruit local talent who better understand market specifics. These employees not only provide valuable local expertise but are also essential for creating authentic connections with regional consumers.

A topic often overlooked by entrepreneurs, which I previously mentioned, is planning an exit strategy. One of the best times to start planning this step is once the company reaches a stage of stability.

Choosing the right exit strategy will depend on the entrepreneur's personal goals, market opportunities, and potential offers from buyers or investors. Some entrepreneurs may wish to remain involved in the business even after a partial sale, while others prefer a complete exit to focus on new projects.

Thus ends this first chapter devoted to entrepreneurial strategy. You are now better equipped to face the challenges and seize the opportunities that will come your way.

CHAPTER 2
GROWTH AND EXPANSION

"What does not kill us makes us
stronger."
Friedrich Nietzsche

The growth of a business is one of the most exciting and challenging aspects of the entrepreneurial journey. However, growth is not just about increasing sales or expanding staff; it must be strategic, sustainable, and aligned with the company's values and mission. In this chapter's introduction, we'll explore the various dimensions of entrepreneurial growth, with a focus on strategies, challenges, and opportunities that arise at each stage.

Growth does not happen in a vacuum. It must be supported by a deep understanding of markets, consumers, and economic trends. This involves careful planning and rigorous execution. As the famous abolitionist and writer Frederick Douglass said, "If you can't explain it simply, you don't understand it well enough." This quote highlights the importance of clarity in growth vision and strategy.

To truly seize growth opportunities, it's essential to start with an objective assessment of the current state of the business. This includes an analysis of the company's strengths, weaknesses, opportunities, and threats, which helps to create a comprehensive overview. This assessment not only helps to identify internal strengths to leverage but also weaknesses to address.

Target markets are at the heart of this analysis. What is the profile of your ideal customer? Which market segments have yet to be tapped? Identifying new customer segments, whether through geography, demographics, or buying behavior, is a crucial step to direct growth efforts.

An example is Nubank, a Brazilian digital bank. At its launch, it identified a massive growth opportunity in traditional banking, which was seen as too rigid and inaccessible for many consumers. By targeting young people and those without access to traditional banking, Nubank was able to grow quickly and sustainably.

Once opportunities are identified, it's time to define a growth strategy. One of the most effective approaches is to diversify the products or services offered. This can mean adding new products, expanding into new regions, or even changing the target market. For example, a cosmetics company might decide to expand its product line to include skincare or perfumes, thereby increasing its appeal to a broader audience.

At the same time, innovation plays a key role in growth. Companies that embrace a culture of innovation are often better prepared to adapt to market changes and respond to emerging consumer needs. By investing in research and development, a business can not only improve its existing products but also create new ones that meet unmet demands.

A well-known illustration of successful innovation is Apple, which reinvented the smartphone market with the iPhone. As we saw in the first chapter, by combining elegant design, advanced technology, and an exceptional user experience, Apple transformed not only its own business model but also the entire tech industry.

It is essential to define key performance indicators (KPIs) to measure growth. These may include metrics such as revenue growth, customer base expansion, or profitability improvement. Regularly analyzing these indicators not only tracks progress but also allows for adjustments to the strategy based on results.

A good example of this practice is Zalando, the online fashion retailer. Over the years, Zalando has carefully monitored its KPIs, which allowed it to identify trends in buying behavior and adjust its offerings accordingly. For instance, noticing a growing demand for ethical and sustainable clothing, Zalando diversified its offerings to include eco-friendly brands.

While growth is a desired objective, it also brings considerable challenges. Managing rapid growth requires strategic planning to avoid pitfalls such as operational overload, dilution of company culture, or loss of service quality. Companies must be ready to adapt their processes, train their teams, and invest in the necessary infrastructure to support growth.

A striking example of this challenge is WeWork, which experienced explosive growth but also had to face internal management issues and a rapid devaluation of its market value. Indeed, the rush to expand at any cost without a solid structure in place led to disastrous consequences.

To support sustainable growth, it is essential to develop a company culture that values innovation, collaboration, and continuous learning. Company culture can be a powerful driver of success. When employees feel valued and motivated, they are more likely to contribute to the company's mission and actively participate in its growth.

A prime example of this philosophy is Google, which has created a stimulating work environment where innovation is encouraged. Google offers its employees the chance to dedicate a percentage of their time to personal projects, which led to revolutionary products like Gmail and Google News. By promoting an environment conducive to innovation, Google has been able to maintain its leadership position in the tech market.

As a company grows, it must also explore new markets. This may involve geographic expansions, entering new customer segments, or even diversifying into new industries. For success, it is crucial to conduct in-depth market research to understand the needs and preferences of consumers in these new segments.

Netflix, transitioning from a DVD rental-by-mail service to streaming and then investing in original content production, anticipated future trends and thus succeeded in positioning itself as a global leader in entertainment. International expansion can represent an immense opportunity for companies aiming to grow. Starbucks is an example of a company that succeeded in its international expansion. By adapting its offerings to local tastes while maintaining its brand identity, Starbucks has successfully entered diverse markets, from China to India. For example, in China, Starbucks introduced drinks suited to local tastes while creating social coffee experiences that resonate with Chinese culture.

As a company grows, it is crucial to keep maintain the quality of its products or services. Rapid growth can sometimes lead to compromises on quality, which can harm brand reputation. To avoid this, visionary entrepreneurs need to establish solid processes and rigorous quality controls.

By embracing the Japanese philosophical principle of Kaizen, or continuous improvement, Toyota managed to maintain high quality standards while growing massively. This focus on quality has helped make Toyota one of the largest automotive manufacturers in the world, with an unrivaled reputation for reliability.

Every entrepreneurial journey is marked by obstacles. For many entrepreneurs, one of the greatest challenges is managing the pressure of growth. The need to meet increasing demand while maintaining efficient operations can create considerable stress. Visionary entrepreneurs must, therefore, be prepared to make difficult decisions and face uncertainties.

An inspiring example is Howard Schultz, former CEO of Starbucks, who faced major challenges during the company's rapid expansion. In times of economic difficulty, Schultz decided to focus on quality and customer experience rather than expansion at any cost. This allowed Starbucks to maintain its reputation and strengthen its market position.

When considering growth, it is essential to pay special attention to optimizing operations. This means closely examining the company's internal processes and identifying areas that can be improved to support rapid expansion. Efficient operations can save time and resources, which is essential as demand increases.

Amazon is a prime example of success in this area. The company has invested heavily in its logistics and supply systems, creating an incredibly efficient distribution network. Through automation, artificial intelligence, and data analysis, Amazon can manage a vast range of products while ensuring fast delivery. This operational optimization has been a key factor in its ability to grow at a rapid pace while maintaining customer satisfaction.

Strategic partnerships can play an essential role in a company's growth. By collaborating with other businesses, entrepreneurs can access new markets, share resources, and benefit from the expertise of other industry players. A good example is Spotify, which has formed partnerships with companies such as Facebook and Uber. These collaborations have enabled Spotify to reach new users and enhance its service offerings. By integrating its services with other platforms, Spotify positioned itself as a leader in the music streaming industry.

In the digital age, data also plays a central role in decision-making. Visionary entrepreneurs must adopt a data-driven approach to understand market trends and anticipate customer needs. Data analysis can provide valuable insights into consumer behavior, allowing businesses to adapt quickly.

Airbnb is a good example. The company uses data to optimize pricing, improve user experience, and target its marketing campaigns. By analyzing booking behaviors, Airbnb has been able to adjust its offerings to meet user expectations, strengthening its position in the market. For sustained growth, companies that want to stay relevant understand they must continuously innovate. This means not only introducing new products or services but also regularly reassessing business models and internal processes. Innovation must be integrated into the company culture to be sustainable.

For long-term success, it is crucial to regularly assess the company's growth. This involves tracking key performance indicators (KPIs) that measure financial results, customer satisfaction, and other relevant metrics. Smart entrepreneurs must be ready to adjust their strategy based on the results obtained. Tesla, for example, closely monitors its KPIs, including sales, customer satisfaction, and production timelines. By using this data, Tesla can make continuous improvements to its operations, allowing it to meet the growing demand for its electric vehicles effectively. With growth comes risk. Visionary entrepreneurs must be aware of potential dangers and put strategies in place to mitigate them. This may involve product diversification, cash flow management, and scenario planning.

CHAPTER 3
OPERATIONS AND EFFICIENCY

"The path to success is paved with
perseverance and hard work."

Booker T. Washington

Operational efficiency is often what separates a stagnant company from one that thrives. Operations are the beating heart of a business, where the management of resources, processes, and capacities determines its ability to grow and adapt to market changes. A careful handling of these elements ensures not only sustainability but also competitiveness in an ever-evolving environment.

Every company, whether a startup or a multinational, must ensure that its internal processes are optimized to achieve maximum results with minimal resources. This means that every step, from acquiring raw materials to delivering the finished product, should be thoughtfully refined to maximize efficiency.

Let's consider Toyota, once again, as a pioneering company in operations management through its Lean production system. This system is based on eliminating waste at every level whether it be time, materials, or human effort. Toyota introduced methods like the Kaizen system, which we've previously discussed, promoting continuous improvement through small regular adjustments. This type of management not only reduces costs but also ensures the quality and consistency of products.

Effective supply chain management is also critical for any business wanting to maintain its competitive edge. A well-managed supply chain not only ensures timely product delivery but also reduces costs, optimizes inventory, and enhances customer satisfaction.

A striking example is IKEA, the furniture giant. IKEA streamlined its supply chain by optimizing each step, from product design to logistics and production. Through a well-organized network of suppliers and rigorous inventory management, IKEA can offer competitive prices while ensuring fast delivery to customers worldwide.

Key performance indicators (KPIs) are essential for monitoring operational efficiency. They enable entrepreneurs to know if processes are on track or if adjustments are needed. These metrics can include elements such as production lead time, manufacturing costs, product defect rate, and customer satisfaction levels.

Zara, a leading company in the fashion industry, uses KPIs to optimize its processes. Zara has developed an extremely responsive production model capable of launching a new collection in just a few weeks, while closely monitoring product quality and customer satisfaction. By continuously measuring and adjusting its processes, Zara has managed to stand out in an industry where speed is crucial.

One of the major challenges in operations management is cost control while maintaining high product quality. This requires the optimal use of human, financial, and material resources. Poor management can lead to waste, reduced quality, and loss of competitiveness.

Southwest Airlines offers a good example of cost control without compromising service quality. The company adopted a policy of fleet simplification, using only one model of aircraft, which significantly reduced training and maintenance costs. Additionally, by minimizing optional services and maximizing flight efficiency, Southwest Airlines has maintained solid profitability, even in difficult economic periods.

Flexibility is essential in a constantly evolving world. Companies must be able to quickly adapt their operations to new market demands, technological advancements, or unforeseen crises. This may involve redefining processes, reassessing partnerships, or integrating new technologies.

The COVID-19 pandemic highlighted the importance of flexibility. Many companies, like Tesla, had to adjust their production lines to meet new conditions. Tesla, for example, temporarily redirected its production to manufacture medical ventilators in response to the growing demand. This ability to quickly pivot operations not only kept Tesla operational but also reinforced its brand image as an innovative and responsive company.

The management of bottlenecks is a major obstacle to operational efficiency. These friction points in processes slow down production, increase costs, and can even affect product or service quality. Identifying and implementing solutions to mitigate these bottlenecks is an essential task for any entrepreneur.

In the automotive industry, companies like Ford have tackled this challenge with ingenuity. When Ford developed the assembly line, it managed to eliminate many traditional bottlenecks in production. By breaking down work into repetitive, specialized tasks, Ford sped up the production time of its cars and lowered costs. Although the assembly line has become a symbol of industrial efficiency, it mainly highlights the importance of rethinking processes to remove barriers that hinder productivity.

Bottlenecks can occur in any industry. They can stem from defective machinery, poor personnel management, or an inability to meet demand promptly. Every entrepreneur must regularly analyze key stages of their business activity to identify slowing points. Specific solutions should then be implemented, such as improving equipment maintenance, providing continuous employee training, or adopting newer, more efficient technologies.

One of the most effective ways to improve operations is by introducing automated systems. These technologies enable the automation of manual processes, thereby reducing human errors and increasing productivity. Automated systems can range from supply chain management software to robots in factories.

For instance, Amazon uses advanced technology to manage its warehouses. Through robotic systems and artificial intelligence software, Amazon can handle massive order volumes with near-perfect precision. Robots assist in transporting goods, while AI algorithms optimize delivery routes and manage inventories. This automation has enabled Amazon to become a major leader in logistics.

Effective operations management also depends on a skilled team. A team that understands the company's goals and possesses the technical skills to manage operations is essential to ensure processes run smoothly. Continuous training, skill development, and engaging employees in process improvement are crucial elements in maintaining operational efficiency.

At GE Aviation, a continuous training program for employees has been implemented. The company invests in both technical and managerial training for its teams to ensure its manufacturing and maintenance processes remain among the best in the industry. By constantly training its employees, GE not only ensures that its operations remain efficient but also that its products maintain the highest quality.

Efficient operations management is the backbone of any company's success. Whether optimizing processes, automating tasks, overcoming bottlenecks, or building a skilled team, each aspect of operations must be carefully planned and enhanced. Operational efficiency not only reduces costs but also enables the delivery of higher-quality products and services to customers, thereby strengthening the company's competitiveness and sustainability.

In the words of Booker T. Washington, "The path to success is paved with perseverance and hard work." It is therefore essential to understand that entrepreneurial success does not rest solely on great ideas or bold marketing strategies but also on meticulous attention to the details of daily operations.

CHAPTER 4
MARKETING AND SALES

"The key to success is to focus on goals,
not obstacles."

William C. Durant

In an increasingly competitive market, attracting and retaining customers is both an art and a science. Entrepreneurs must continuously adjust their strategies to capture the attention of their target audience while strengthening relationships with existing customers. This requires a deep understanding of consumer behavior and the ability to respond quickly to changes. The first step is to clearly define your ideal customer. Who are they? What problems are they looking to solve? What are their desires, motivations, and constraints? The more you understand your audience, the better you will be able to align your offering with their specific needs.

A common mistake entrepreneurs make is believing that everyone is a potential customer, while in reality, success often comes from precise segmentation and targeted attention. To illustrate this point, consider a brand of natural cosmetic products. Instead of targeting all beauty consumers, this brand chooses to specifically address customers who are concerned about sustainability and the environment. By adjusting its messaging, it can not only attract a more engaged audience but also develop stronger loyalty because its values align with those of its customers.

Once you have identified your ideal customer, the next challenge is to maintain their interest. Retaining customers often costs less than acquiring new ones, but it requires constant effort. Providing quality service, establishing a relationship of trust, and continuing to innovate are essential elements for keeping your customers engaged in the long term.

To succeed in marketing, it is imperative to measure the return on investment (ROI). Too many entrepreneurs spend money on advertising campaigns or initiatives without a clear vision of their profitability. Every euro spent should generate measurable value for the business. ROI helps determine which initiatives actually provide value and which require adjustments or cuts. This could include analyzing sales generated by a specific campaign, customer acquisition costs, or tracking social media interactions. With modern tracking tools like Google Analytics, entrepreneurs can now access precise data for each campaign, allowing them to continuously optimize their strategies.

An effective method is to establish key performance indicators (KPIs). For example, if you launch an email marketing campaign, you can track KPIs such as open rates, click-through rates, and conversion rates. These data will allow you to adjust your email content, sending frequency, and even segment your mailing lists for better results.

The world of marketing is evolving at a dizzying pace, particularly with the advent of digital technologies. What worked five years ago may be obsolete today. Therefore, entrepreneurs must be agile and ready to adjust their strategies at any moment. Consumer behaviors are changing rapidly, influenced by many factors: economic crises, social trends, technological advancements, and more.

For example, the rise of social media has radically changed the way consumers discover and interact with brands. It is crucial to monitor these trends and understand how they influence the customer journey. A business that relies solely on traditional marketing methods could quickly find itself outpaced by more dynamic and responsive competitors.

The Nike brand has successfully adapted its strategy over the years. Rather than focusing solely on television advertising, the brand quickly became familiar with new digital platforms like Instagram and YouTube to engage younger consumers. It has also implemented initiatives around influencer marketing, collaborating with athletes and personalities who embody the brand's values. The result? Nike continues to dominate the sports apparel market by constantly adapting to new market realities.

An effective marketing strategy also relies on choosing the right channels to reach your customers. It can be tempting to want to be present everywhere, but this can quickly dilute your efforts and resources. It is essential to focus on the channels that generate the most value for your business. Every company must evaluate channels based on its specific objectives and target audience.

For example, a B2B company might find that LinkedIn and webinars are very effective channels for generating leads, while a fashion brand might achieve better results by investing in Instagram, TikTok, or even partnerships with influencers. The key lies in experimentation: it is often necessary to test several approaches to see which ones yield the best return on investment.

Furthermore, cross-channel communication has become an essential trend. The idea is to provide a consistent experience across different touchpoints. If a customer discovers your brand on Instagram, interacts with a Facebook ad, and then places an order through your website, the experience must be seamless and fluid. By offering continuity in your messaging and interactions, you enhance customer engagement and retention.

For example, a startup selling eco-friendly products might focus its marketing efforts on Instagram to raise awareness among a young audience, then use email campaigns to offer personalised promotions to website visitors. By uniting these channels under a common vision, the startup can not only attract customers but also convert these prospects into loyal buyers.

In terms of sales, it is crucial to understand that the act of purchasing is the result of a series of positive interactions between the customer and the brand. Transforming a prospect into a customer, and then into a brand ambassador, requires constant efforts in service, follow-up, and user experience. Personalization plays a crucial role here.

The era of mass marketing has evolved into a growing demand for personalization. Consumers expect experiences that speak directly to them, tailored to their individual preferences. Using customer data to better segment and personalize offerings can be a significant competitive advantage. Companies that invest in this approach often see higher conversion rates and increased loyalty.

For instance, Amazon excels in personalizing product recommendations based on users' browsing and purchasing histories. This type of personalization maximizes cross-sell and upsell opportunities. Companies adopting similar strategies can not only increase their sales but also enhance the customer experience.

Another key element of customer retention is creating an emotional connection with your customers. This can be achieved through shared values, an authentic brand story, or exceptional customer service. Offering loyalty programs, discounts for repeat customers, or simply attentive post-purchase follow-up can make a significant difference in long-term customer retention.

The sales landscape has radically changed over the past few decades. Online sales, social media, and evolving consumer expectations have pushed companies to constantly innovate in their sales approaches. Today, an entrepreneur must be prepared to face more informed and demanding customers. Therefore, it is essential to train sales teams on these new realities and adopt tools that facilitate customer relationships.

Moreover, sales cycles can vary depending on the industry. Some businesses, particularly in the B2B sector, have long and complex sales cycles, requiring a strategic approach to maintain the prospect's interest at every stage. This could include product demonstrations, personalized follow-up calls, or even sending informative and relevant content throughout the decision-making process.

To maintain this engagement, the key is to remain proactive. Being attentive to prospects' signals, anticipating their needs, and offering solutions before they even ask for them is vital. Additionally, using effective customer relationship management systems allows tracking of every interaction, keeping a history, and personalising the next steps.

A marketing strategy, no matter how innovative or creative, must prove its effectiveness in terms of tangible results. This is where the concept of return on investment (ROI) comes into play. With ROI, the profitability of marketing actions is measured by comparing the costs invested in a campaign with the benefits generated. For entrepreneurs, understanding and mastering this indicator is essential to maximize profits after evaluating what works in their marketing strategy.

Each marketing channel or initiative must be accompanied by rigorous analytical tracking. When done correctly, data analysis can reveal hidden trends, underutilised market segments, or even inefficiencies in marketing resource allocation. For example, a company investing in a Facebook Ads campaign might compare the total campaign cost to the revenue generated by customers who interacted with that ad. If the campaign generates a positive return on investment, it justifies continuing to invest in that channel. Conversely, if the return on investment is negative, it may indicate that an adjustment or change in strategy is necessary.

Tracking metrics is also important for measuring the conversion rate (the percentage of prospects that become customers), customer acquisition cost (CAC), and customer lifetime value (CLV). These key indicators allow entrepreneurs to adjust their campaigns in real time, optimize budgets, and maximize the impact of every dollar spent.

However, ROI is not always limited to immediate figures. Some initiatives, like branding or creating value-added content, may take time to show results. Therefore, it is crucial to distinguish between short-term and long-term strategies, assessing the impact of both on the overall growth of the business.

In a world where consumer preferences and behaviors are constantly evolving, visionary entrepreneurs must be able to adapt quickly. What works today may become obsolete tomorrow. That's why it is essential to stay attuned to the market and emerging trends in order not to be caught off guard.

Data and technology provide a window into these changes. Analyzing consumer behaviors on your website, interactions on social media, or even search trends on Google can indicate shifts in customer preferences. This information allows for rapid adjustments to offerings, modifications to marketing messages, or the launch of new products aligned with emerging needs.

Take the rise of mobile commerce as an example. In recent years, purchases via smartphones and tablets have seen exponential growth. A business that does not take this trend into account could lose a significant share of its market. Adapting your website to be mobile-friendly or even developing a dedicated app can be a key factor in maintaining consumer engagement and converting them into buyers.

Furthermore, changes in how consumers perceive brands also play an important role. New generations, in particular, are placing increasing importance on ethical values, sustainability, and corporate transparency. Entrepreneurs must be prepared to integrate these values into their marketing and business practices to stand out in an increasingly competitive market.

Finally, an often underestimated but extremely powerful tool in marketing is storytelling. Telling an engaging and authentic story can create a deep emotional connection with your customers. Instead of simply selling a product or service, a company can position itself as an essential player in the lives of its customers by sharing stories that resonate with their values and aspirations.

The story you tell must align with your brand identity. For example, if you offer eco-friendly products, sharing the challenges faced in making your supply chain more sustainable can strengthen the connection with your customers. Major brands like Apple, Nike, or Tesla have mastered the art of storytelling. They do not just sell products; they sell a vision. Buying an iPhone means entering the Apple universe, with its promises of innovation and creativity. Purchasing a pair of Nike shoes brings you closer to the spirit of self-improvement that the brand embodies.

Small businesses can also leverage storytelling, particularly by sharing their entrepreneurial journey. Narrating how the business was founded, the obstacles overcome, and the successes achieved can inspire customers and lead them to support a brand they perceive as authentic and aligned with their own ideals.

CHAPTER 5
FINANCE AND FUNDING

"There is nothing more dangerous
than to enter into business without
knowing what you are doing."
Benjamin Franklin

Financial management is an essential foundation for
entrepreneurial success. Understanding cash flow,
investment strategies, and financial risks is crucial
for building a prosperous business. In this fifth chapter,
we will explore these key aspects in depth, drawing
inspiration from best practices and historical examples.

Financial management begins with a clear understanding
of basic terms and concepts. Every entrepreneur must
master the following notions:

• Balance Sheet: A balance sheet is a financial statement
that presents a company's financial position at a specific
point in time. It shows assets, liabilities, and equity,
allowing entrepreneurs to assess their net worth.

• Income Statement: This document presents revenues
and expenses over a given period, helping to evaluate the
profitability of the business. A detailed income statement
helps identify sources of revenue and control expenses.

• Cash Flow: Monitoring cash flow is crucial to ensure the company's liquidity. This involves analyzing inflows and outflows of funds to ensure that the business can meet its financial obligations.

The first step for any entrepreneur is to establish rigorous accounting and use financial management software to track these indicators. This not only helps to meet tax obligations but also aids in making informed decisions.

A well-developed budget is the cornerstone of financial management. It serves as a plan for strategically allocating resources. Here are some steps to create an effective budget:

1. Identifying Expenses: Categorize all business expenses (fixed and variable) to have an overview of costs.

2. Forecasting Revenues: Estimate future revenues based on past performance and market trends. This includes considering seasonality and economic fluctuations.

3. Safety Margin: Include a safety margin in the budget to address unforeseen events and avoid financial crises.

4. Regular Monitoring: The budget should be a living document, reviewed regularly to adjust to economic realities and business performance. This allows for quick responses to variances.

Entrepreneurs must be cautious in their investment decisions. J.P. Morgan, for example, was known for his diligence in evaluating investment opportunities. Here are some investment strategies to consider:

• Diversification: Don't put all your eggs in one basket.

Diversifying investments helps to reduce risks.

• Thorough Research: Before investing, it is crucial to conduct detailed research on companies or sectors. Understanding the market and trends can make the difference between success and failure.

• Long-term Investments: Prioritise investments that can generate income over the long term rather than seeking quick gains.

Cash flow management is essential for maintaining a company's financial health. Here are some key practices:

1. Cash Flow Forecasting: Establish monthly cash flow forecasts to anticipate financial needs. This helps avoid unpleasant surprises.

2. Receivables Management: Implement clear credit policies to ensure customers pay on time. This includes sending reminders and setting up discounts for early payments.

3. Cost Reduction: Identify areas where costs can be reduced without compromising quality. This may include negotiating with suppliers or optimizing internal processes.

Finally, financial analysis is indispensable for making informed decisions. Entrepreneurs should always use key performance indicators (KPIs) to assess their financial situation. Here are some essential KPIs to track:

• Profitability Rate: Measure profitability relative to investments made. This helps evaluate the effectiveness of implemented strategies.

• Liquidity Ratio: Assess the company's ability to meet its

short-term obligations. This helps identify potential problems before they become critical.

• Trend Analysis: Observe financial trends over multiple periods to anticipate the company's evolution.

Prudent financial management, inspired by figures like J.P. Morgan, can ensure entrepreneurial success. By asking the right questions and implementing effective strategies, visionary entrepreneurs can successfully navigate the business world.

CHAPTER 6
LEADERSHIP AND TEAM

"I want to be myself, not conform
to what others expect of me."

Harriet Tubman

In business, leadership plays a crucial role in creating a high-performing team. A good leader inspires not only through their skills and vision but also through their authenticity. Harriet Tubman, an emblematic figure in the civil rights struggle, embodies this quality. Her affirmation of wanting to be herself, rather than conforming to the expectations of others, reminds us that authenticity is a strength.

Leaders who encourage their teams to embrace their authenticity cultivate a work environment where employees feel valued and respected. This creates a culture of openness and collaboration, which is essential for innovation and performance. By being themselves, team members are more likely to share their ideas, take on responsibilities, and contribute to collective success.

A visionary leader understands the importance of

recruitment in building a strong team. Choosing the right people for the right positions is essential, but it is equally crucial to seek individuals who share the organization's values. During the recruitment process, leaders should ask questions that allow candidates to express their authenticity and passion. This ensures that each team member contributes uniquely to the collective mission.

In an era where remote work is becoming the norm, leaders must adapt their management methods. Maintaining employee motivation from a distance requires clear and regular communication. Leaders should create opportunities for team members to connect, share their successes, and tackle challenges together. By fostering a culture of trust and transparency, they enable everyone to express themselves freely, without fear of judgment.

The example of Harriet Tubman also illustrates the importance of empathy in leadership. She guided hundreds of people to freedom by listening to their needs and supporting them in their struggles. Similarly, a visionary leader must listen to team members, understand their challenges, and encourage them to overcome obstacles.

The performance of a team relies on the diversity of talents and ideas. Leaders must foster an environment where everyone feels comfortable contributing. By integrating different perspectives, they stimulate innovation and creativity. This may also involve continuous training and professional development to help each member reach their full potential.

Moreover, effective leadership relies on the ability to inspire and motivate while allowing each individual to remain true to themselves. By following the example of leaders like Harriet Tubman, every manager can guide their team toward authentic success, where everyone contributes meaningfully and feels proud to be part of the organization.

Another essential aspect of leadership is performance management. Evaluating the performance of each team member not only helps identify areas for improvement but also recognises exceptional contributions. Regular recognition, whether formal or informal, motivates employees and strengthens their commitment to the company. Visionary leaders have always been able to recognise the strengths of those they guide. They understand that each individual has a unique role to play in their quest for collective success. By celebrating small victories and acknowledging everyone's efforts, leaders can build a sense of belonging within their team.

For a team to be high-performing, it is crucial to promote collaboration. Leaders should create opportunities for team members to work together on projects and initiatives. This not only strengthens interpersonal relationships but also encourages an exchange of ideas that can lead to innovative solutions. Team-building activities, such as workshops or retreats, can also help establish stronger connections among members. These shared experiences allow everyone to better understand their colleagues, learn to work together, and align on common goals.

Conflicts are inevitable in any team, but how a leader manages them can make all the difference. Rather than ignoring tensions or taking sides, a good leader should approach conflicts constructively. This means listening to all parties involved, understanding their perspectives, and working to find solutions that benefit everyone.

Conflict management is also a learning opportunity. By addressing issues openly, leaders show their teams how to resolve disputes in a healthy manner, thus reinforcing communication and problem-solving skills within the team.

The company culture is a direct reflection of leadership. A leader must be aware of the values and behaviors they promote, as these directly influence employee engagement. By embodying the company's values and leading by example, leaders can establish an environment where everyone feels empowered and committed. A strong sense of belonging is essential for employees to feel motivated to give their best. Leaders can encourage this culture of engagement by creating open communication channels, regularly soliciting feedback, and showing that they value each team member's contributions. A good leader also knows that they should not only focus on team results but also on the personal development of each member. This involves providing opportunities for training, mentoring, and coaching. By investing in the professional development of employees, leaders ensure that everyone has the tools necessary to succeed and grow within the organisation. Personal growth is essential for maintaining an engaged and motivated staff. Employees who feel supported in their development are more likely to remain loyal to the company and contribute to its success.

CHAPTER 7
TECHNOLOGY AND DIGITAL TRANSFORMATION

"The technology should enhance
human life, not replace it."

Dave Waters

Today, technology plays a crucial role in the efficiency and competitiveness of businesses. The integration of technological tools not only improves processes but also reduces costs and maximizes resources. However, understanding how to leverage technology without losing sight of human aspects is a critical skill for any entrepreneur.

From data management to task automation, the digital age has introduced unprecedented solutions to simplify operations. However, not all technologies are suitable for every business. Here, we will explore how to identify, integrate, and optimize technological tools to enhance efficiency while keeping human balance at the core of your business strategy.

Choosing the right technological tools is the first step to ensuring efficiency in a business. The market is full of solutions and innovations, ranging from customer relationship management (CRM) systems to enterprise resource planning (ERP) systems, not to mention collaborative tools. But how do you know which tools to adopt?

It is crucial to understand your specific needs before investing in new technology. For example, if your business struggles with inventory management or human resources, an ERP solution such as an inventory management platform may be appropriate. Similarly, platforms like Slack or Microsoft Teams can enhance communication within your team, especially in a remote work environment.

When selecting a technology, consider its scalability. Solutions should adapt to the growth of your business without requiring constant revision of your systems. Take Amazon, for example, which has invested heavily in automation and logistics technologies to remain competitive while managing millions of orders each day.

One of the greatest advantages of technology is automation. Automating repetitive tasks allows your team to focus on higher-value tasks. Processes such as invoicing, payment management, or lead tracking can be handled by automation software, saving hundreds of hours of manual work.

Automation also helps reduce human error, thereby improving the accuracy of operations. For example, companies like Uber automate their payment and driver management processes, reducing margins for error while enabling smoother and faster transaction management. However, automation should not replace human judgment; rather, it should support process optimisation without dehumanising interactions with customers or employees. The balance between technology and human relationships remains a key factor for success.

In the digital age, cybersecurity has become an essential priority for any business. Data breaches can not only compromise the security of sensitive information but also harm a company's reputation and lead to significant financial losses. Therefore, it is imperative to integrate robust cybersecurity measures from the outset.

The first step is to conduct a risk assessment to identify vulnerabilities in your system. Use cybersecurity tools to monitor and protect your data, such as firewalls, antivirus software, and intrusion detection systems. Additionally, training employees on best security practices is essential. They must be aware of potential threats, such as phishing, and know how to respond in the event of a suspected attack.

Companies like Target and Equifax have suffered major data breaches, severely impacting their reputations. By investing in appropriate security measures, businesses can avoid these disasters and ensure customer trust. This contributes to a company culture where data security is valued, thereby enhancing the brand's reputation and reliability.

The world of technology is evolving at a breakneck pace. It is therefore essential to stay abreast of emerging trends and be ready to adopt innovations that can provide a competitive edge. This means being attentive to new technologies such as artificial intelligence, data analytics, and the Internet of Things (IoT).

Businesses must regularly evaluate their technological strategy. Participating in conferences, reading specialized publications, and engaging in professional networks are effective ways to stay informed. For example, tech giants like Google and Apple invest heavily in research and development, allowing them to stay at the forefront of innovation.

The adoption of new technologies, however, must be carried out strategically. For example, integrating artificial intelligence into customer service can transform the user experience, but it also requires careful planning to ensure that implementation goes smoothly. By thoroughly assessing the needs and impacts of each new technology, companies can avoid costly mistakes and maximise their return on investment.

Artificial intelligence (AI) and machine learning are transforming the business landscape. These technologies enable companies to analyse massive volumes of data, identify trends, and optimise decision-making processes. For instance, e-commerce companies use AI algorithms to personalise the shopping experience, which can significantly increase conversion rates.

AI can also enhance operational efficiency. For example, AI-powered automation tools can manage tasks such as demand forecasting or inventory management, allowing businesses to operate more effectively. However, it is essential to ensure that these technologies are implemented with an ethical approach, considering their impact on employment and human decision-making. Companies must also be prepared to invest in training their employees to fully leverage new technologies. Continuous education and skill development are crucial to ensuring that employees are equipped to work with advanced tools and understand the implications of AI in their field.

CHAPTER 8
INNOVATION, RESEARCH AND DEVELOPMENT

"Imagination is more important
than knowledge."

Albert Einstein

As we all know, innovation is the spark of economic growth and sustainable development. In a constantly evolving world, where technologie advance at an exponential rate, companies must adopt an innovation mindset to remain competitive. What is innovation? It is a process by which new ideas, products, or services are developed and brought to market. Successful companies are those that understand that innovation is not limited to creating new products but also includes improving existing processes and finding creative solutions to consumer problems.

Part 1: Types of Innovation
Innovation can be classified into several categories:

1. *Product Innovation*: This involves developing new products or improving existing ones. Take the example of

Tesla, which has revolutionized the automotive industry with its electric cars. Their innovation lies not only in battery technology but also in user experience and autonomous driving systems.

2. *Service Innovation*: This form of innovation focuses on improving the services offered to customers. Companies like Airbnb have redefined the hospitality sector by providing a platform that connects travelers with hosts, thus transforming the traditional travel experience.

3. *Process Innovation*: This concerns optimizing production or delivery methods. Companies that integrate technologies such as automation or artificial intelligence into their business processes, like Amazon with its advanced logistics, gain significant competitive advantages. In summary, innovation is essential to meet the ever-evolving needs of consumers and to differentiate oneself in the market. The ability to innovate is what allows a company to thrive in a dynamic business environment.

Part 2: Research and Development:

The Engine of Innovation Research and development (R&D) is the process through which companies invest in innovation. Investing in R&D is crucial for creating new products and improving existing ones. A company that neglects R&D risks stagnation and losing market share to more innovative competitors.

Take Apple, for example, which allocates a significant portion of its revenue to R&D. This level of investment

enables it not only to develop new products, such as the iPhone and Apple Watch, but also to continuously improve its existing ecosystem, like the iOS operating system. Through these efforts, Apple has managed to establish a loyal customer base that is eager to adopt its new innovations as soon as they are launched. Companies must also be willing to take calculated risks in R&D. Failure is an integral part of the innovation process. Sometimes a product may not achieve the expected success, but the lessons
learned from that failure can lead to even more significant innovations. For instance, the Google Glass project was a commercial failure, but it paved the way for further developments in augmented reality.

To support R&D, companies should also establish strategic partnerships with universities, research centers, or other businesses. These collaborations can provide access to additional resources and expertise that can accelerate the innovation process. Companies that adopt this approach are often better positioned to capitalize on technological advancements.

Part 3: Fostering an Innovation Culture:

Creating an environment conducive to innovation is essential for stimulating creativity within a company. Leaders must encourage their teams to explore new ideas and take initiative. An innovation culture is built on trust, where employees feel comfortable sharing their ideas without fear of judgment.

Companies can encourage innovation in several ways:

1. *Encourage Risk-Taking*: Employees should feel safe to experiment with new ideas. Companies that adopt an approach that values failure as a learning opportunity foster an innovation mindset.

2. *Provide Resources*: Equipping employees with the tools and resources to develop their ideas can stimulate innovation. For example, some companies establish innovation budgets or mentorship programs to help employees bring their ideas to fruition.

3. *Foster Collaboration:* Encouraging collaboration between different teams can lead to innovative ideas. Inter-team brainstorming sessions can generate creative solutions by combining diverse perspectives.

4. *Celebrate Successes*: Recognizing and rewarding employees who contribute to innovative projects can strengthen motivation and inspire others to think creatively. Cultivating an environment conducive to innovation allows companies not only to generate new ideas but also to retain employees who feel valued and engaged.

In the age of information and technology, innovation and research and development have become imperatives for companies wishing to succeed. The future of innovation depends on companies' ability to adapt and anticipate the changing needs of consumers. For visionary entrepreneurs, innovation is more than just a tool; it is a philosophy to be integrated into every aspect of the business.

Imagination, as Albert Einstein said, is more important than knowledge, as it is the key that opens the gateway to new possibilities. Entrepreneurs must not only invest in R&D but also encourage a culture of innovation within their organizations. By integrating innovative strategies, they can create products and services that meet customer expectations while surpassing the competition.

CHAPTER 9
WORK-LIFE BALANCE AND PERSONAL WELL-BEING

"Never let somebody tell you you can't do
something. If you have a dream, you have
to protect it."
Will Smith
(In The Pursuit of Happyness)

The balance between work and personal life is a crucial issue for entrepreneurs. In a world where professional demands seem unending, it is easy to lose oneself in work at the expense of mental and physical well-being. The importance of a good balance cannot be underestimated, as it contributes to productivity, creativity, and personal satisfaction. As a visionary entrepreneur, you must recognise that your overall well-being is directly linked to your personal and professional success.

To avoid burnout, it is essential to establish clear boundaries. Working relentlessly does not always lead to better results; on the contrary, it can lead to decreased motivation and performance. By setting working hours and sticking to them, you ensure that you have time to recharge. Regular breaks allow you to return to work with a clear mind and renewed ideas. By incorporating relaxation moments into your schedule, you not only improve your well-being but also boost your creativity and problem-solving ability. Stress management is also essential for maintaining this balance. I recommend reading this 2 books: The Four Agreements" by Don Miguel Ruiz.

This bestseller provides a philosophical approach to reducing stress through four simple principles, such as not taking things personally and avoiding assumptions. The second book: Meditation for Everyday Life" by Christophe André.

Entrepreneurs often face stressful situations that can feel overwhelming. To manage this stress, practices such as mindfulness, meditation, or yoga can be very helpful. Taking a few minutes each day to focus on the present moment can reduce your anxiety level and improve your concentration. My secret formula against stress is to often repeat these words as a mantra: "Balance" or "Zenitude."

Moreover, setting priorities in your work is an effective strategy for managing stress. By classifying tasks by urgency and importance, you can better control your workload and avoid feeling overwhelmed.

Staying motivated is another fundamental aspect of work-life balance. Motivation can fluctuate, but there are several strategies to maintain it. One of the most effective is to set clear and achievable goals. These goals provide you with direction and allow you to measure your progress. Additionally, by celebrating your successes, even the small ones, you reinforce your motivation.

Surrounding yourself with inspiring people is also beneficial. Sharing ideas with other entrepreneurs can rejuvenate you and encourage you to pursue your dreams with great determination. Investing in personal development is another way to stay motivated and improve your well-being. By learning new skills, reading books, or participating in training, you broaden your horizons and boost your self-confidence. This also prepares you to face challenges and changes that arise in the business world. Task prioritisation plays a key role in effective time management and stress reduction.

By adopting time management techniques, such as the Dwight D. Eisenhower Matrix or the Francesco Cirillo Pomodoro Technique, you can structure your day to optimise your efficiency. These methods help you stay focused on important tasks while avoiding work overload.

Learning to say no when necessary is also a valuable skill. Entrepreneurs must be aware of their limits and know when it is time to step back to recharge. Taking care of your mental well-being is essential for an entrepreneur. Dedicating time to activities that promote overall well-being, such as hobbies, exercise, or socialising, is crucial. Spending time in nature, for example, can significantly improve your mood and help you disconnect from daily pressures.

The balance between work and personal life is a key element of entrepreneurial success. By adopting strategies to manage stress, stay motivated, and develop your skills, you can enhance your productivity and overall well-being. Remember that success is not only measured in terms of financial results but also in terms of personal satisfaction and well-being. As Will Smith's quote reminds us, it is crucial to protect your dreams and not let anyone discourage you. By emphasising this balance, you give yourself the best chance to thrive both professionally and personally.

The balance between work and personal life is a critical issue for entrepreneurs. Too often, the passion for their business can lead them to sacrifice their personal time, health, and well-being. As an entrepreneur, it is very important to understand that your effectiveness does not rely solely on the number of hours you work.

A good balance is essential not only for your own health but also for the long-term success of your business. First, establishing a regular schedule and sticking to it is a good starting point. By creating a routine, you can better manage your time and reduce stress related to unforeseen events. This includes setting clear working hours as well as planning time for personal activities, whether it's spending time with family, friends, exercising, or simply relaxing. This structure helps you stay focused during work hours and fully enjoy your leisure moments.

In addition to organising your time, it is crucial to find stress management strategies that work for you. Every entrepreneur is different, and what works for one person may not always work for another. This may include practices like mindfulness, meditation, regular exercise, or even hobbies that you are passionate about. The important thing is to find ways that help you disconnect and refocus. It is also beneficial to stay motivated by surrounding yourself with positive people.

Your network plays a key role in your motivation. Attending networking events, joining entrepreneurial groups, or even engaging with mentors can provide you with support and inspiration. These interactions can not only strengthen your determination but also offer new perspectives on challenges you may face.

An entrepreneur who values their achievements is more likely to approach future challenges with a positive attitude. Task prioritisation is essential for effectively managing your time. An effective approach is to use time management tools that help you organise your tasks according to their importance and urgency. This strategy not only increases your productivity but also reduces the stress associated with tight deadlines. It is crucial to remain flexible and adjust your priorities as unexpected situations arise.

One of the biggest challenges for entrepreneurs is not to become overwhelmed by work. This can lead to mental and physical fatigue, even burnout. To avoid this, learn to say no to projects or tasks that do not align with your priorities. This cultivated quality allows you to maintain a healthy balance and ensures that you invest your time in what truly matters to you.

Mental well-being is often a neglected component of personal well-being. It is imperative to dedicate time to activities that promote your overall well-being for the sake of your business. This can be as simple as spending time with friends, reading a good book, or engaging in an artistic activity. These moments of disconnection allow you to recharge your batteries and approach your work with a fresh mind.

In summary, maintaining a balance between work and personal life is essential for any visionary entrepreneur. It requires constant attention and a willingness to prioritize not only your work but also your health. By cultivating this balance, you position yourself not only for success in your business but also for leading a fulfilling and satisfying life.

The balance between work and personal life is an essential concept that every entrepreneur must consider. In a dynamic and competitive business environment, it can be easy to get swept away by professional demands. However, it is crucial to remember that success is not solely about work performance; it also encompasses physical and mental well-being.

To establish this balance, it is vital to develop a daily routine. This routine should include working hours as well as dedicated moments for relaxation and personal activities. Establishing clear boundaries between work and personal life helps avoid burnout and maintain consistent productivity. An entrepreneur who knows when to stop and rest is better prepared to face significant future challenges.

As you have explored these chapters, you have delved into essential pillars for building a sustainable and prosperous business. Each step, strategy, and principle discussed in this work forms the foundation upon which the journey of any visionary entrepreneur rests. These lessons, born from reflection and knowledge, are addressed to those who dare to dream big and act accordingly.

Now, it is time to take a step back to assess these insights and transform them into concrete actions. Before concluding, let us remember that entrepreneurship is, above all, a journey toward personal as well as professional growth.

CONCLUSION
THE VISIONARY ENTREPRENEUR'S

"Success is not the key to happiness.
Happiness is the key to success. If you love
what you do, you will succeed."
Albert Schweitzer

Entrepreneurship is more than just a job. It's a mindset, a way of seeing and shaping the world around you. On the path of entrepreneurship, it's essential to remember that every challenge, every apparent failure, is actually just a disguised opportunity to learn, grow, and get a little closer to success.

If you have read this book up to this point, you now know that the path to entrepreneurial success is never linear. It is marked by highs and lows, brilliant successes and painful defeats. But what sets a visionary entrepreneur apart from another is the ability to persevere, to rise after each fall, and to constantly reinvent one's approach.

My own journey reflects this reality. From a childhood marked by adversity to a long period of homelessness and then imprisonment, I learned that the key to success does not lie solely in knowledge or technical skills but in resilience and determination. This book, along with the one I published on the Amazon platform, "The Codes of Stoicism: The Black Book & 9 Keys to Access the Circle of Winners," reflects this journey a path where every obstacle is an opportunity to become better, stronger, and wiser.

As entrepreneurs or future entrepreneurs, you are the architects of your own future. You hold the power to improve not only your life but also the lives of others through your innovations, ideas, and leadership. The world of entrepreneurship will demand sacrifices, patience, and a lot of courage, but it will also offer you invaluable rewards: the freedom to create, to lead, and to impact the world in your own way.

Remember the words of Will Smith: "Don't let anyone tell you you can't do something. If you have a dream, you must protect it." This quote perfectly embodies the spirit of this book. You are responsible for your dreams, and it is up to you to nurture, protect, and turn them into reality, no matter the obstacles you encounter along the way.

I leave you with this thought: entrepreneurship is not simply a way to make a living. It is a commitment to yourself, to your vision, and to the impact you wish to have on the world. And even if you have not yet started a business, know that you are already on the right path because entrepreneurship begins in the mind before manifesting in the real world.

May this book guide you, inspire you, and push you to be the best version of yourself. The world needs optimistic visionaries, and you are one of them.

Books to Deepen Your Knowledge on Leadership, Growth, and Entrepreneurship:

1. *"The Lean Startup"* by Eric Ries
 • A must-read reference on creating and developing a startup with an agile, learning-centered approach.

2. *"Good to Great"* by Jim Collins
 • A guide on what distinguishes a good company from an exceptional one.

3. *"Zero to One"* by Peter Thiel
 • A unique take on innovation and how to build companies that create new things.

4. *"The Innovator's Dilemma"* by Clayton Christensen
 • A classic on how companies can continue to innovate in changing environments.

5. *"Start with Why"* by Simon Sinek
 • A book exploring the importance of having a deep sense of purpose in everything one undertakes, starting with the "why."

6. *"The E-Myth Revisited"* by Michael E. Gerber
 • This book debunks the myths of entrepreneurship and provides a method to transform a small business into a high-performing enterprise.

Websites and Blogs:

1. Entrepreneur.com
• A comprehensive site with articles, advice, and resources for entrepreneurs at all stages of their journey.

2. Inc.com
• A site dedicated to startups and growing businesses, offering advice on everything from funding to leadership.

3. HubSpot Blog
• Articles on marketing, sales, and customer service, with a particular focus on growth strategies for businesses.

4. The Startup by Medium
• A blog on Medium that features entrepreneurs' stories, practical advice, and thoughts on innovation.

5. Seth Godin's Blog
• The blog of Seth Godin, a marketing expert, offering daily advice on creativity, leadership, and entrepreneurship.

6. Y Combinator Startup Library
• Free resources from the Y Combinator accelerator for entrepreneurs, with guides and videos on starting and managing startups.

7. Harvard Business Review
• Academic and practical articles on business management, leadership, and innovation.

8. Neil Patel Blog
• A blog focused on digital marketing and online business growth, with tips for optimizing traffic and conversions.

Combined with the insights shared in this book,

"Leadership and Growth: The Visionary Entrepreneur's book," these resources will allow you to continually enrich your skills and entrepreneurial knowledge, helping you become not only a successful entrepreneur but also a visionary leader in an ever-evolving world.

About the Author:

Rūmī Abdoūlatīf is an author passionate about personal development, success, science-fiction.

After facing significant challenges including a period of homelessness and time in prison, I discovered powerful tools in Stoicism and meditation that helped me radically improve my life.

My first book, Stoicism Codes: The Black Book & 9 Keys to Access the Winners' Circle, published on Amazon, draws on the knowledge I gained through extensive reading during my incarceration. This work explores the fundamental principles of Stoicism as well as practical strategies for achieving success both personally and professionally.

With Leadership and Growth, I aspire to inspire entrepreneurs whether beginners or experienced to overcome challenges and seize opportunities in their professional lives.

Follow me on Instagram and sign up on my website to receive the latest articles published on my blog.

Contact:
- Instagram: @RumiAbdoulatif • TiTok: AbdoulatifRumi
- Website/Blog: www.payhip.com/BloomingLightSquare

www.ingramcontent.com/pod-product-compliance
Lightning Source LLC
Chambersburg PA
CBHW052327220526
45472CB00001B/316

*9 7 9 8 3 0 0 3 2 2 8 7 8 *